LIFE LESSONS TODAY FROM THOSE WHO PLAYED YESTERDAY

JUST ASK

21 DEVOTIONS FOR THE GIRL WHO LOVES SPORTS

SARAH ROBERTS

Just Ask

ISBN 978-1-938254-42-0

Cross Training Publishing
www.crosstrainingpublishing.com
(308) 293-3891

Photo Credits:
Jennie Finch photo credits: Landon Finch and USA softball
Laura Clay: David Smith
Shannen Fields: Tara Stone
Becca Clark: Shevaun Williams
Kelli Masters: Kevin Jairaj
Leah Amico: Josh Menashe and Franco Bagattini
Samantha Ricketts: Mississippi State Media Relations
Andrea McHugh: Matt Cashore and Michael Bennett
Misti Cussen: ORU Media Relations
Caitlin Way: Clay Billman
Minta Spears: Texas Tech Athletics Communication
Arkansas: University of Arkansas Media Relations
University of Oklahoma: Ty Russell
Sherri Coale: Jack Newhouse
Facing the Giants: used by permission of Sherwood pictures with photo credit by Bob Scott

Table of Contents

Dedication   5

Preface   6

Foreword   7

Just Ask Joseph   9

Just Ask the Disciples   13

Just Ask the Israelites   17

Just Ask David   21

Just Ask Jesus   25

Just Ask Samson   29

Just Ask Zacchaeus   33

Just Ask John the Baptist   37

Just Ask Rahab   41

Just Ask the Samaritan   45

Just Ask Shadrach, Meshach and Abednego   49

Just Ask Mary and Martha   53

Just Ask Paul and Silas   57

Just Ask Ruth   61

Just Ask Esther   65

Just Ask Isaiah   69

Just Ask Jesus   73

Just Ask Judas   77

Just Ask Paul   81

Just Ask Gideon   85

Just Ask the Boy   89

Dedication

*T*his book is dedicated to my love, my coach, my best friend, and my husband. Chris, I love how you love me. You have hurt when I have hurt. You have celebrated when I have celebrated. You have believed in me when I didn't believe in myself. Your leadership and love for our family amaze me. I am proud to be your wife! I love you!!

Acknowledgements

To my dad, Gary Riffe: I have a relationship with my heavenly father because of the influence, leadership, and love of you, my earthly father. Thank you for being my greatest coach! I love you.

To my mom, Sherri Riffe: You taught me what it means to love your children unconditionally and to serve unselfishly...all in the name of Jesus! You are the greatest mom in the world! I love you!

To Stacey and Stephanie: I am so thankful that I can say my sisters are also my best friends. Thank you for giving me truth when I needed it and love when I wanted it. I love you all so much! To Cale, My Heart: There is no one that has a bigger heart than you. You teach me so much by how you love others! I love you! To Chloe, My Joy: There is no one that makes my heart smile as much as you. You bring me so much joy that my cup overflows ! I love you! To Case, My Light: You are the light of my life! I light up every time I see you, hug you, and kiss you with lipstick on! I love you! To Elisha, My Hope: You have been through so much in your little life that I look at you and see hope. Jesus loves you and so do I! To Christian, My Peace: You are the perfect example of doing life with Jesus isn't the absence of problems but the presence of peace. I am so proud of the man you are and honored to be your adopted mom. I love you! To Jim and Kathryn: Thank you for being the best in-laws a girl could ask for! So thankful for all your love and support! To My CWP (Coaches' Wives Posse): Shannon, Julie, and Penny: You girls have laughed, loved, and gotten me through some fun and difficult times with your prayers and encouragement!! I love doing life with you all! Love you so much!

To Stefne Miller, Donna Noonan, and Chuck and Kay Harrison: Thank you for all the times you let me borrow your belief.

To Gordon, Cross Training Publishing, and Jeff Martin: Thank you so much for believing in this project! You all have been so awesome to work with!

To my Oklahoma FCA Family: You all are the best teammates! I am honored to come alongside you and influence the State of Oklahoma for Jesus.

Thank you to all the women who shared their stories for this book. I am inspired by your bravery, courage, and hearts for Jesus! You all are world changers!

Preface

*"He comforts us in our troubles so that we can comfort others.
When they are troubled we will be able to give them the
same comfort God has given us."*
1 Corinthians 1:4

I want to surround myself with people who are doing life and doing it with the help of our God. In Proverbs 20:18 it says, "Plans succeed through good counsel; don't go to war without wise advice."

Girls, we are in a war: A war over our bodies, a war over our teammates, and a war over our hearts. We need all the good counsel and wise advice we can get. I love that we serve a God that understands this and created a book of peoples' stories to help us get through ours.

We have this entire book, God's Word, that is dedicated to helping us get through the up and downs of this one life we have been given. I want to challenge and encourage you to open your Bible, grab a pen, and ask God to speak to you through the stories you read. Allow a personal God to get personal with you.

As a girl who loves sports, you are going to hear from some amazing women I love and have learned from myself. They will inspire you and encourage you with their hearts and testimonies. I am so thankful they allowed me to share their stories with you! It is my prayer for you, as you read these stories that it helps you write your own. We each have a story that needs to be written and shared for those that come behind us. After all, that's what history is....HIS— Story. I am so excited to be a small part of yours as you understand that you are a huge part of God's.

Foreword

*A*s a high school teacher, coach and Thursday night FCA Huddle Group Leader, I used to sit on my fireplace hearth with my three-year-old son in my lap while the quarterback of our football team played his guitar, leading my house full of adolescent athletes in the singing of "Our God is an Awesome God." If a young mother could receive any bigger boost than the casting of that vision on the impressionable mind of her child, I don't know what it would be. I remember thinking at the time that FCA had a marvelous way of working forward and backward and inside out.

Those of us fortunate enough to be a part of FCA through the years have all found that we get from it more than we could ever give to it. It is a vehicle that opens doors to those who don't know God, and it is a vehicle that gives a power surge to those who do. When the narrow road gets hard to navigate and the expectations of the world loom large, it is the fellowship of Christians that keep us going.

Through 30 plus years in the world of women's sports at both the high school and the college level, I can attest to the unique challenges Christian women face. God didn't make us the same inside or out. We don't look alike, we don't feel alike, and we don't think alike. A godly woman's path is a long and winding road filled with unexpected crooks and bends. More than once I've wondered aloud if I couldn't just get a sign or two to help me along the way.

None of us has all the answers. We're lucky if we even get the questions right most of the time. But we itch, all of us do. And daring to scratch that itch by asking hard questions is so, so important. We have much to learn from those who have gone before, especially those whose roads are catalogued for us in the Good Book. But sometimes, especially when we're stretched and spent, the lessons can seem hard to find. 'Just Ask' pairs the lessons of the Bible with the dilemmas of our world, and if you haven't found yourself pondering each and every one of these questions just yet, I promise you, you will. Your day is coming.

Sarah Roberts is an angel of FCA. She's also a wife and a mother and a sister and a friend. And she itches with questions, too, just like we all do. So much so that she decided to start writing them down. And then she asked, and she asked and she asked. And now she's sharing what she found out with all of us.

These little devotions flash like neon way finders scattered by the hand of God. So comforting to remember we're all in this together, and we can help each other find the way home.

Enjoy the Journey.
Sherri Coale

There are times God allows the losses to prepare us for the wins…

Just Ask Joseph

Read Joseph's story: Genesis 37, 39-45

As a competitor, you never, I mean never, enjoy losing. It is the losses that cause the anger, the hurt, and the disappointment. If you look at a picture of the mountains, you will notice the growth doesn't happen on the mountain tops, but in the valley. The biggest growth as an athlete and a person doesn't happen in the wins but in the losses. Joseph understood this all too well because he went through a lot of losses. His losses included the loss of his family when he was sold into slavery and the loss of his freedom when he was thrown into prison for a crime he didn't commit. But even after all that, Joseph knew God was in each loss and was using each one of them to mold and make him into the person and leader God wanted him to be. When Joseph finally met up with his brothers, he said,… "do not be angry with yourselves for selling me into this place. It was God who sent me here ahead of you to save your lives…he is the one who made me an advisor to Pharaoh—the manager of his entire palace and the governor of all Egypt." That's right, the losses led him to be the governor of all of Egypt and that's a pretty big win. And he knew that even in the losses God never left his side. In the pain, God was still there. In the trials and hard times, God was still there. In each and every loss, God was still there. He was there making Joseph into the leader of Egypt that God wanted him to be. Joseph's experience with loss should encourage you in yours. So whether you are experiencing losses with your team or losses in your life, like a friendship or a loved one, know that God can and will work through each and every one of them, teaching you lessons of hope, perseverance, and patience. The Bible teaches us in Romans 8:28, "God works all things to the good for those who love him and are called according to his purpose." Did you catch that? "All things to the good"…all things includes the losses in our life. He is walking with you through each one of them, molding and shaping you into the girl and athlete God wants you to be.

9

Just Ask Jennie Finch
Olympic Gold Medalist • USA Softball Team

*I*t was my sophomore year at the University of Arizona. The season before had been fine, but I had higher expectations for myself. I had to get better. I expected to be the best I could be.

After a great start to the season, we traveled on April 21, 2000 to take on our biggest rival, the Arizona State Sun Devils. I was pumped that Coach gave me the ball to start the Pac-10 season. It was my time to prove that I deserved to be in the circle. Everyone in the state gets fired up for this match up. We had a 30 plus game winning streak against them. It was always a pitchers' duel.

It was a flat pitch I threw over plate in the bottom of the seventh inning that quickly became the game-losing home run. I was crushed more than the ball that travelled over the fence. This wasn't supposed to happen. I had let down my team, coach, our fans, former players and myself. The winning streak was broken, and I was devastated.

After a quick pick up of our stuff we rushed to the bus; I was disgusted with my performance and the outcome. I saw my mom and dad and hugged them. I remember burying my face in my dad's chest and telling him, "Dad I never want to lose again. I never want to have this feeling again." His reply was, "You are the person God knew could handle this." I got on the bus for what seemed like the longest bus ride of my life back to U of A. I was at my lowest of lows as a player. I can remember so many thoughts and negative feelings in my mind and body. This was by far the biggest loss of my career.

Sometime in 2007, many years after that lowest night of my Wildcat career, my dad randomly asked, "Jen, do you remember that loss to ASU?" My reply, "Yeah, of course dad. Thanks for bringing it up!" "Did you know that loss was the beginning of your 60 game winning streak?" my dad said. I was shocked. I had no idea.

At times we can be at our lowest of lows. In those times it's difficult to see beyond the end of the day or the trials we face. We don't have the ability to see beyond our present circumstances. We don't, but God does.

Just Ask Me

1) What has been your hardest loss as an athlete?

2) What has been your hardest loss as a person?

3) What have you learned from your greatest losses?

*"You are my rock, my salvation, and my fortress.
I will not be shaken."*
Psalms 62:6

God will use storms to show us He is in control...

Just Ask the Disciples

Read about the disciples' storm: Matthew 8:23-27

One of the greatest storms an athlete can face is that of an injury. If you have been an athlete very long, you understand the disappointment, the fear, the anger that comes with an injury. You have worked so hard to get prepared for your season and one wrong turn or one wrong move, and you are out for a period of time watching everyone else get better. You are facing a storm just like the disciples. The disciples found themselves on a boat in the middle of the sea, in the middle of a storm, and Jesus was asleep! The waves were hitting the boat and they were scared...so are you. The wind was blowing them over and they were overwhelmed...so are you. They felt like Jesus wasn't awake to hear their cries...so do you. Like the disciples, you just can't understand why Jesus would be sleeping on the job. Doesn't he know you are in trouble? Doesn't he know you are in a storm? Doesn't he know that you are in pain? Yes, he knew all those things when he was in the boat with the disciples, and He knows that now with you. Like the disciples, however, our faith is not found in our circumstances, but in Jesus. We spend so much time focusing on the storm instead of the one who controls the storm. God uses these storms in our lives to bring us closer to him and rely fully on his control of the situation. In John 5:17, Jesus says "My Father is always working, and so am I." When we ask God, "What are you doing?" His answer will always be "I am working."

We may be worried, but we need to know God is working. We have to understand there is no wasted pain, there are no wasted tears, and there are no wasted storms. He will use every single one of them to build our faith in him and bring about something good that we could never think or imagine. After Jesus calmed the storm that day, the Bible says the disciples "were amazed." Their faith in Jesus grew that day in the midst of a storm, and God wants your faith to grow today in the midst of yours.

Just Ask Sherri Coale

Head Basketball Coach • University of Oklahoma and Team USA

*W*e could have had Sinatra singing "High Hopes" at our beginning of the 2012-2013 season team meeting. I've never walked into a space that felt so capable. It was like all our guys were wearing moon shoes and Final Four capes. They had belief in bold dreams dripping off of them. And it wasn't pie in the sky. We had all the pieces and we had all the parts. It was one of those years that had "meant to be" written all over it.

Except that it wasn't. Meant to be that is. At least not in the way we had imagined.

On an otherwise uneventful early October practice, our starting post player snapped her left Achilles, the first of four season-ending catastrophes that would leave us with eight players, a mere shell of the squad that had floated around the room in August.

One was a freshman prodigy, one a sophomore starter, one a seasoned senior, and the other our heart and soul.

After the first two, I thought I could fix it. I was devastated, of course. But I thought I could find a way anyway. This was my job, to lead when my team needed to be led, to press on when they would be inclined to falter. "I can do this" was my daily mantra. And press on we did, though our fragile pieces and parts were strung together by a thread.

But the third one was different. If the first two were right and left hooks to the chin, this was a sucker punch to the soul. It took my breath away. I was scared. I was confused. I didn't get it. And though I had been praying all along the way, the nature of my prayer changed that afternoon.

I can't tell you that I asked for strength any differently, or that I asked for direction I had not been pleading for, but something about my insides was different when I talked to God that day. I had run out of me, and that made room for so much more of Him. Hallelujah.

Because of that, I could absorb—and thus WE could absorb—the final blow of this treacherous streak of injuries. When our 'heart and soul,' the final of the four, went down, I didn't panic because Jesus was sleeping in the bottom of the boat; I knew He was in charge. That made taking those early steps across the water easy.

We just stared at him and put one foot in the front of the other. Ultimately, our band of warriors walked straight into the Sweet 16. We did what we could with what we had, but we let Jesus run the show. And like always, He takes us where we're supposed to go.

Just Ask Me

1) What storms are you facing in your sport and/or life today?

2) How does the story of the Disciples storm encourage you?

3) Write a prayer to God asking him to show himself to you during this storm in your life.

"For I know the plans I have for you, says the Lord. Plans to prosper you not to harm you, plans to give you a hope and a future."
Jeremiah 29:11

Failure is never trying…

Just Ask the Israelites

Read the Israelites story: Numbers 13 and 14

*H*ave you ever wanted to not play a game because you knew you weren't going to win? You were already defeated before the game ever began. You failed in your mind before your body ever tried. Let the lesson of the Israelites be an encouragement of what not to do when you face an opponent you don't think you can defeat. God sent the Israelites to fight an enemy, a giant enemy, and take over the land. This was land he said he was "giving them." That's right….the God of the universe promised them this land. He promised them a win, yet they never got to experience it because they chose to focus on the Giant and not God. It sounds crazy to us, right? Wouldn't you believe the God of the universe? If God is for you who could be against you? What could giants do to you when you have God telling you, "I'm giving you this land." It's sounds crazy, yet we do it ALL the time.

Jesus said, "I have come so that you may have life and have it to the full." (John 10:10) That is our promised land: and life to the fullest, more than we can ever imagine. But then there are the Giants.....

- *Giants of fear*
- *Giants of depression*
- *Giants of disappointment*
- *Giants of regret*
- *Giants of discouragement*
- *Giants of doubt*
- *Giants of failure*
- *Giants of being overwhelmed*
- *Giants of thoughts of inadequacy*

We focus on giant after giant, all keeping us from entering the promised land of life to the full. One of the keys to victory in the sports world is to listen to your coach each time you face a giant on the court or field. The same goes for this life. When facing these giants of life focus on the words of your head coach, "In this world you will have trouble. But take heart! I have overcome the world." John 16:33

Just Ask Shannen Fields

Brooke Taylor • *Facing the Giants*

God can use anybody He wants, anytime He wants, anywhere he wants! God showed me this a few years ago when I had so many doubts like the Israelites. Early in my life I had a tendency to believe and speak negative thoughts about myself. I certainly didn't believe God could use a country girl from a small town. I had no college degree. Despite being blessed with a great marriage and two beautiful children, there was a void in my life. I could see my husband reaching others through his football coaching, but I didn't believe my life would ever impact others with any significance. This story began in my late twenties when I was asking God to use me more. My problem was that I was approaching my dreams without fully surrendering them to God. I was determined to make my own path. I had a desire to do things that was much larger than myself. I know God put those desires there, but I didn't trust Him fully to take the reins of my life. I set off to do it my way. My husband and I moved from my small hometown to a larger city. My plans were to get an agent and makes things happen in the film world. I wanted to be in movies. Fast forward a year, and nothing had happened the way I had planned. The self-doubt began to creep back into my life. "I will never amount to anything" and "I'm just an ole country girl that will never accomplish anything," are words I began to believe. I didn't see myself as God sees me. God needed me to trust him and believe I could defeat these giants of fear and self-doubt. He needed me to know that He had already ordered my steps. I just needed to walk in them. It took time before I found myself giving my hopes and dreams to Jesus. I began to surrender my desires to Him first. Before I had been directing my path, but now I was allowing God to be "The Director." I even told God that I didn't have to be in movies. I only wanted Him and His joy in my life. When I finally allowed God to direct, something really amazing began to take place in my life. I thought God could never use me. I thought God was limited to a place. I thought God needed a perfect person. I put God in a box! God opened a door for me to be cast as the lead female role in a nationwide Football Film called *"Facing the Giants"* Wow! God can really use anybody He wants, anytime He wants, anywhere He wants! The secret of life is letting go and letting God. Trust is hard when you can't see the bigger picture but the Lord makes firm the steps of the one who delights in him. (Psalm 37:23) and my favorite *"Delight yourself in the Lord and he will give you the desires of your heart."* (Psalm 37:4)

Just Ask Me

1) Name a time in your life you wanted to quit before you ever competed in the game.

2) Write down the giants that keep you from living a full life with Jesus?

3) Look in God's Word for the promises that will defeat these giants.

"Let us then approach God's throne of grace with confidence, so that we may receive mercy and find grace to help us in our time of need."
Hebrews 4:16

When you feel overlooked by people, you are being seen by God…

Just Ask David

Read David's story: 1 Samuel 16: 1-13

One of the negatives of being a girl is how we can be so negative. So often we think we aren't good enough, smart enough, or pretty enough. We will tear ourselves down starting with our face, body, personality, and athletic ability until there is no self-esteem left. And when there is nothing left of ourselves, we move on and tear others down next. We want to be seen by the world when we are seen by the one who created it, God. David understood what it felt like to be overlooked by people. When his father was asked to bring his sons before the prophet Samuel so he could choose the next King, David's father brought all the sons except David. He left David to watch the sheep. David wasn't the oldest. He wasn't the biggest. He wasn't the most athletic looking, but God warned Samuel, "People judge by outward appearance, but the Lord looks at the heart." (1 Samuel 16:7b)

After Samuel asked if there were any more sons, David's father brought David before Samuel. God said 'that's the one, the man after my own heart.' David was made the future King of Israel not because of what he looked like on the outside but because of who he was on the inside. When David was overlooked by people he was seen by God, and so are you! You may feel overlooked by your coach, your parents, or your teammates, but God sees your heart.

When we ask God to change our hearts, he ends up changing our eyes too. We were once blind, but now we see. We see ourselves how God sees us and we see others how God created them….all in His image.

Just Ask Andrea McHugh
Notre Dame • Volleyball

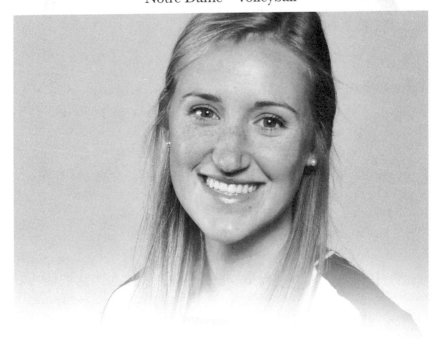

*I*t was during my junior year of high school in 2009 when my dad wanted me to go to a national volleyball tryout. In total, there were about 7,000 girls trying out for a 12-team roster. "Dad, this is silly! I'm not good enough; there is no way I'll make it." If any of you play volleyball, you know that a 5-foot-10 outside hitter is considered short in volleyball and probably not good enough to play at division one, so you might as well just become a libero already. I knew that the coaches wouldn't even take a look at me because of my size, and I knew I simply wasn't going to beat out the best players in the country. No way!

I love my dad for a number of reasons, and one of them is his ability to bring out the best in me. My dad has a way of making me think that I can do anything because he knows what I am capable of doing. However, I tend to ignore his compliments and encouragement because he has to say that, right? He is MY Dad! But after all maybe he is right.

So, I went to the tryout thinking I was just going to embarrass myself, but at least I would get better. One of the things I love about our God is that He has a sense of humor. During the tryout one of the coaches commented on my bright pink nail polish, which immediately put a smile on my face and eased away my worries for the rest of the tryout.

Well, I ended up making the 20 roster training team. We trained for about a week at the Olympic Training Center in Chula Vista. At the end of training camp, the roster would be cut down to 12. At training camp, I had decided that no matter what, I was going to walk away from the last practice knowing I left everything on the court. The night the coaches called out the final 12 team roster, I could barely breathe I was so nervous. I remember praying and just saying, "Your will be done." The coaches were getting down to the end of the list and I heard, "Andrea McHugh." I was jumping for joy on the inside! I could barely contain myself! That night when I called my parents to tell them of the exciting news my Dad said, "See I told you you were good enough: I am so proud of you!"

Just Ask Me

1) Record a time you felt overlooked by people around you.

2) How did you respond to this feeling? Did it make you try harder for your coach, walk away from your sport or friends?

3) How does David's experience encourage you today?

"You see me when I travel and when I rest at home.
You know everything I do."
Psalm 139:3

*A*t one time or another, every athlete experiences a slump. You can't make a shot to save your life. You haven't had a hit in 10 games. You just can't seem to make a putt. "The slump" can make us doubt our ability and lead to asking God some hard questions. Why me? What did I do wrong? There has to be something I am doing wrong to cause nothing to go right…right? Well, I want the story of Jesus being led into the wilderness to encourage you as you walk through yours. The Bible says in Matthew 4:1, "Then Jesus was led by the Spirit into the wilderness to be tempted there by the devil. For forty days and forty nights he fasted and became very hungry." Jesus did nothing wrong, yet he was in a wilderness. Jesus did nothing wrong, yet he was tempted by the enemy. Jesus did nothing wrong, yet he was hungry. We learn that God allows us to face trials, not because we have done anything wrong, but to show us His ways are always right. We can trust Him in the wilderness, or the slumps, like Jesus did. We can trust that during these times God may not be building our careers, but our character. He may not be lighting up your stat sheet, but He is igniting your faith. So when you face the slumps of your sport or a spiritual wilderness in your life, don't ask why, but what. God, what are you teaching me? God, what can I learn from you? Remember, God is not interested in growing your fans but His followers, and sometimes that means leading us into some slumps.

Just Ask Misti Cussen
Head Women's Basketball Coach • ORU

*I*n the early fall of my freshman year in high school, I knew had arrived. I received an invitation from our varsity coach to play up that year, joining an upperclassmen-led team, and I was so excited. However, circumstances beyond my control would temper that excitement. That fall, I was diagnosed with bilateral dysgerminoma, a form of ovarian cancer. The surgery necessary to remove it would take away my ability to have children later in life, but at the time I was probably more irritated that I would miss six weeks of basketball! My season ended up being limited to playing with my freshmen squad, but I knew as a Christian that the Lord would have better days ahead.

Fast forward to the fall of my junior year in high school—I was a returning starter from my sophomore season, had already received several college scholarship offers, and I believed that my health issues were behind me. In the last of a series of follow up tests from my freshman year, I was diagnosed with a recurrence of cancer. And, this time surgery wasn't the answer. I would need to undergo at least six months of chemotherapy. With my doctors, family, coaches, and teammates all on board, we scheduled chemo sessions around the basketball schedule. I played my junior season of basketball completely bald and pretty worn down, but I knew in my heart that it was what the Lord was calling me to do and that He would supply my strength and encouragement.

Two years later, I headed off to college on a full ride, but the effects of the chemotherapy would stay with me. The chemicals used in my treatments had dried up the collagen that keeps your tendons and ligaments pliable, and I would experience four ACL tears throughout my junior and senior seasons. My career as a player would come to a premature end, and I experienced an identity crisis. In my quiet times with the Lord, I would question what good could possibly come from such a dramatic, roller coaster career. What about the positive influence I could have had as a Christian athlete and role model? Though I was confused and disappointed, I knew the Lord was in control of my circumstances. I just needed to trust Him regardless of my feelings.

Just Ask Me

1) How do you handle the slumps in your sport?

2) How do you view God when you struggle in your sport or in your life?

3) How does Jesus' story in the wilderness encourage your faith?

"So do not fear, for I am with you; do not be dismayed, for I am your God. I will strengthen you and help you; I will uphold you with my righteous right hand."
Isaiah 41:10

God given talent can be ruined by man-made pride…

Just Ask Samson

Read Samson's story: Judges 16:1-30

*W*e live in a world that suffers from a disease, a disease that has taken many gifted and talented people down. It's a disease that has been known to destroy teams and individuals no matter the race, gender, or sport. It's called the "me disease;" you may know it as pride. We have all been given gifts and talents by God, for God, to do great things because of God. Unfortunately, these God given talents can be ruined by our man-made pride. Samson was given an amazing gift, the gift of strength. God gave him this gift to fight for God's people and against the enemies of God, to rescue Israel from the Philistines. But Samson's pride got in the way. Pride is the "feeling of superiority: a haughty attitude shown by somebody who believes, often unjustifiably, that he or she is better than others." Yes, Samson had a gift. Yes, Samson had an amazing talent, and yes he was the strongest man in the world, but he forgot who made him that way. When his focus became on himself and what he wanted instead of God and what God wanted, he failed. We are tempted so often in sports to give into the disease of pride. We can lead the team in points and find ourselves getting mad when our teammates don't pass us the ball enough. We can get jealous of the praise of others on our team and tear them down with our own words. We get a bad attitude because we believe our playing time isn't what it should be. We forget we have the privilege of playing the sports we love because God wants to use our talents for His glory….not ours.

Samson's story doesn't end because he failed. No, he prayed "Sovereign Lord, remember me again, O God, please strengthen me just one more time" and God did. God wants us to be confident when we step out on our fields and use our gift and talents the best we can; after all He gave them to us.

Just Ask Patty Gasso
Head Softball Coach • University of Oklahoma

I grew up going to church with my family on holidays and an occasional Sunday. It was something I did not look forward to very much because I felt services were boring and hard to follow. As I entered my early teenage years, I would flip channels on the TV (back then we had no remote!) and would find myself stopping the channel any time I saw Billy Graham at the pulpit. I would only do this in private because my family would hassle me to turn the channel. Any time I heard Billy Graham preach I felt he was speaking directly to me, like he knew what was going on in my life. I just didn't know what to do with his words.

As I entered college, I met my soon to be husband Jim and knew he was the man I would marry. We had a problem though. We came from different religions and knew we had to believe as one, as a couple. Like Samson, I had to learn to surrender to God, and I praise the Lord for allowing me to let my guard down. It took me a while to connect with a new church and a new way to worship. Comfortable seats? Casual dress code? Not sure this was for me! It took about two years to figure out that God was a loving and forgiving God, that he has an unconditional love for me, and I felt him calling me to him. I finally learned what it meant to have a personal relationship with the Lord. I could pray and talk to him whenever and wherever I wanted. I was also in search of receiving the Holy Spirit and didn't understand what that entailed. It was preached in the sermons that when you finally surrender your life to Christ, you will feel the Holy Spirit enter into your heart. I had no idea what this meant, but I wanted it to happen to me. Not long after this discovery, I was coaching at Long Beach City College and we were playing a game in Fullerton, California. I was in the third base coaching box and as I was rounding a player from third to home plate, I felt the Holy Spirit take me over. It was such an undeniable feeling that I had been waiting for. I wanted to share it from the mountain tops…I finally understood that I am a child of God and the Holy Spirit was ready to lead my walk. This was one of the most amazing feelings and I will remember it forever, because it changed my life forever.

As a Christian and a softball coach, I understand my role. My job is to be a disciple for the Lord, to share my heart and open the door in young peoples' lives in hope that they will ask the Lord into their heart. I have learned that our God does not care so much that I win games, but that I try to win hearts for Him. This discovery has allowed me to surrender my fears and stress and trust the path that the Lord has for me.

Just Ask Me

1) Write about a time where pride got in the way of your gift, talent, or sport?

2) How can you use your talent to bring God glory?

3) Like Samson, write a prayer asking God to help you play for him in your sport.

"Seek first the Kingdom of God and his righteousness and then all these things will be given to you as well."
Matthew 6:33

There are times we have to put ourselves in a better position to see Jesus in order to experience him…

Just Ask Zacchaeus
Read Zacchaeus' Story: Luke 19:1-10

*U*sually the first question after you tell someone you play a sport is, "What position do you play?" We take pride in our positions as a pitcher, point guard, or goalie, but there are times our coach will ask us to change our position based on our opponent, our team dynamics, or just for a change. A change in position gives us a different look. Zacchaeus experienced this with his very first encounter with Jesus.

Zacchaeus was not a well-liked man as the chief tax collector, but one day he heard about this man named Jesus who was coming by and he wanted to see him. Unfortunately, God did not bless Zacchaeus with height, and he was too short to see Jesus. He could have given up and gone back to his normal life, but he didn't. He changed his position in order to see Jesus and ended up experiencing him.

We often want to experience Jesus, hear from Jesus, and see Jesus working but get frustrated when we don't. Maybe God is wanting us to change our position.

- *Change your position and make God the center of your relationships.*
- *Change your position and wake up earlier so you can spend time with God.*
- *Change your position and look for him in what you watch, listen to, and read.*

That day, Jesus saw Zacchaeus in the tree, called him by name, and went to his house for dinner.

When the world called Zacchaeus a notorious sinner, Jesus called him by his name not his reputation. We can all get caught up in trying to find ourselves in what we do as an athlete or lose ourselves in what we have done as a person. Zacchaeus experienced the love of God that he had never experienced before and he was changed. "…Zacchaeus stood before the Lord and said, *'I will give half my wealth to the poor, Lord, and if I have cheated people on their taxes, I will give them back four times as much!'* Luke 19:8

We, too, can be changed with that same love and experience with Jesus. Jesus can change our perspective when we change our position. Zacchaeus climbed a tree… maybe we should hit our knees.

Just Ask Minta Spears

Texas Tech • Basketball

I graduated high school in May 2012, and a few days later I found myself moving into my college dorm at Texas Tech University. I was extremely excited to start school and begin my collegiate basketball career.

For me, the transition from high school to college was a tough one. As far as basketball went, it was a whole new world. Practices were harder and more intense, and I learned there was a huge time commitment to be a student-athlete. Apart from the basketball side, I also struggled with homesickness and being away from my family.

The first game of the season came, and we were playing at Arizona State. I was really excited because I was getting playing time as a true freshman and was starting to understand the game more.

We built a 10 point lead in the second half, and I got put in to take care of the ball for the win. There was about 1:55 left in the game, when I stepped on my defender's foot as I was doing a dribble move and tore my ACL.

The first thing that crossed my mind was that I had survived summer workouts, pre-season, and homesickness for what? All to get injured in the first game of the season? I was so mad and frustrated because this was not a part of my plan. I kept having this bad attitude until my coach came up to me after the game and whispered Romans 8:28 in my ear.

She helped put things in perspective. I finally realized I was not thinking about anyone beside myself. I was so concerned about my plan and what I thought was best for me that I did not take into account the big picture. I've always believed God has a plan for my life, and my coach helped remind me of that.

Looking back, I can see that tearing my ACL was definitely a blessing in disguise. I found my identity was in Christ, not in basketball. Basketball is a tool God has given me to impact and reach people around me. Through this experience, I've really learned to trust God's plan and purpose for my life.

Just Ask Me

1) How would you react if the coach asked you to change positions in your sport or job?

2) In your own words, how did Zaccheaus' heart change when he encountered Jesus?

3) Pray and ask God if there are some things you need to change in order to see him better. Write them down.

"Search me, O God, and know my heart; test me and know my anxious thoughts. Point out anything in me that offends you, and lead me along the path of everlasting life."
Psalms139:23-24

We can't defeat our opponent if our battle is with our teammates...

Just Ask John the Baptist
Read John the Baptist's story: John 3:22-36

As competitors and girls, we size up our competition from the moment we lay eyes on them. Are they faster than me? Are they taller than me? Are they better than me? We've played out the entire game before it ever begins. This carries over to our team relationships as well. Is she getting more playing time than I am? Is she prettier than me? Does she have more "likes" than me on Instagram? So often, we can't even begin to defeat our opponent on the field because we are fighting with our teammates off the field. The quickest way to ruin a team is to focus on an individual. And before you start thinking about all the girls who do just that….stop! We (and yes, that means you too) can all get caught up in the "selfie" world. I want the example of John the Baptist to encourage you to be the best teammate and friend you can be. John was a preacher who baptized people when they turned to God and told them about a man that would save them named Jesus. When it came time to start his ministry, Jesus asked John to baptize him. One day John's friends came to him and said, "Rabbi, the man you met on the other side of the Jordan River, the one you identified as the Messiah, is also baptizing people. And everybody is going to him instead of coming to us." (John 3:26) Both Jesus and John had disciples who followed them and their teachings. Both Jesus' and John's disciples baptized people who came to them, but only one was the Messiah and John knew it wasn't him. John replied to their jealous and selfish attitude, "…I am filled with joy at his success. He must become greater and greater, and I must become less and less." (John 3:29b). John knew his role on the team, and it was to make Jesus' name known. He put the Kingdom of God before himself. Can you imagine your team if everyone had joy at someone else's success? If everyone put the team before themselves? It starts with you!

Just Ask Stefanie Mahaley
Bethel University • Volleyball

*W*e were getting ready to start our 2010 season, and our team could not have come together any more perfectly. We were all on the same page with where we wanted our season to go, and we knew without a doubt that we would accomplish our goals. I was extremely excited and found myself falling into a leadership role. I was eventually voted as a captain, and from that moment I knew I needed to be the person that every one of my teammates could look up to, both on and off the court.

As the season progressed, our team progressed. We were beyond excited to play in our first tournament of the season. I had a pretty off day. I couldn't put any ball down for a kill. So I was subbed out for my best friend on the team, who just so happened to be a freshman. She played great. I remember being super proud of her. That quickly wore off when we played our second, third, fourth and fifth match and I had no playing time whatsoever. I tried to be happy because we won the tournament, but I couldn't help but to feel somewhat bitter.

The more we played, the more I didn't play. My frustration grew stronger and stronger to where I began distancing myself from my closest friend and team. I was no longer myself, and everyone could see it. I felt so inadequate and useless. How did it look for a freshman to be starting over an upperclassman who happened to be a captain. I started comparing myself to her and became jealous. I decided I was not going to sit around and pout for the rest of the season. My sole purpose no longer was about my team reaching our goal but it became me proving myself in spite of my friend. One day, she got injured. As soon as I heard, I was ecstatic. I finally got my chance in a game and I balled out. The entire time I was using my anger toward my teammate to fuel my fire. When it was over I saw her and had this "yeah, that's right" attitude toward her, but she came to me and gave me the biggest hug and said "I'm so proud of you. I'm happy you finally got your shot."

I completely broke. All this time I had built up so much anger toward this person who truly cared for me. And all I could think about was myself. Even after I had treated her the way I did, she was sincerely happy for the team and me, completely selfless. I was so wrapped up in myself that I missed out on opportunities to fulfill my true role as the firecracker on the team.

The Kingdom of God is our team. We can accomplish so much for Christ and His kingdom if we fulfill the roles we've been given, and support our teammates in theirs.

Just Ask Me

1) Name a time when you were jealous at someone else's success.

2) How can jealousy ruin a team, friendship, or relationship?

3) How does John the Baptist's attitude encourage you in yours?

"But love your enemies, do good to them, and lend to them without expecting to get anything back. Then your reward will be great..."
Luke 6:35

Just because you have a past doesn't mean you don't have a purpose...

Just Ask Rahab

Read Rahab's Story: Joshua 2:1-24 and Hebrews 11:1-3, 31

One of the hardest aspects about participating in sports is the mental element of the game. So many times we miss a shot and are scared to take another one. Our passes haven't been on target, and we start thinking too much. We haven't had a hit in the last five games, or fell the last time we attempted a cheerleading stunt and are scared to try it again. These are just some of the examples we face in our sports where things that happened in our past can affect our purpose the next day or the next play. We can learn from Rahab that our past doesn't have to determine our future in sports or in life. Rahab actually worked as a prostitute, but made a choice one day to help men of God. Because she chose to do this, she soon became a follower of God. God didn't see her past as an issue of how he wanted to use her and you shouldn't see yours either. When the world saw a prostitute, God saw a girl. When the world saw a prostitute, God saw a purpose. When the world saw a prostitute, God saw a plan. We learn that God used this girl with a past to change the future for all humanity. Rahab is actually the 28th great grandmother of Jesus and made her way into the hall of fame of faith in Hebrews 11! Just like Rahab, God isn't concerned with your past, but He is concerned with your future. You might be struggling with a past disappointment in your sport or a past disappointment in your life, either one God wants you to know that your past doesn't determine your purpose. This day, God wants you to come to him with your past so that together you can be brave and accept the future he has for you; a future that may consist of forgiveness for your past, strength for the next play, or bravery to try again.

Just Ask Caitlin Way

Oklahoma State University • Track

Growing up, I was a victim of sexual abuse. As a result, I spent a good portion of my life feeling ashamed, dirty, damaged, and guilty. Even though I wasn't the one at fault, I still felt responsible for what happened to me. And although my family attended church every Sunday and I knew about God, I didn't think there was any way God could love me, let alone have any use for someone like me in a part of his plan. So in high school, I gave up on God and put myself on the bench.

It wasn't until I got to college that I finally understood who God really was. He opened my eyes and allowed me to see His relentless and ridiculous love for me, the kind of love that would send His only Son to die for me so I could spend and eternity with Him. Now that's not a God who saw me as dirty, damaged, and guilty… that's a God who saw me as pure, whole, righteous, and redeemed. He always saw me and loved me as the woman I could become, not the girl I thought I was. The challenge was just getting me to see it and believe it.

Once I started believing I was who God said I was and not who I thought I was, the shame started to fade away. My confidence started to grow, and God started to show me He could use my messy past to help other people. Through FCA, he gave me numerous opportunities to share my story with others and watch Him reach them through me. This helped me realize the passion I have for ministry and ultimately led me to my current job, ministering to college athletes every day as a coach.

It took every bit of my 24 years, the good, the bad, and the ugly to get to where I am today. God can and will use us, not in spite of where we have been… but BECAUSE of where we have been. All we have to do is surrender, believe, and walk in the faith that we are who He says we are.

Just Ask Me

1) Read Philippians 3:13-14: "Brothers and sisters, I do not consider myself yet to have taken hold of it. But one thing I do: Forgetting what is behind and straining toward what is ahead, I press on toward the goal to win the prize for which God has called me heavenward in Christ Jesus."

What is in your past that you just can't seem to get past? A choice? A play?

2) What do you need to do today to press on towards your goal and future?

3) Write a prayer asking God to help you with your past. You may need to ask for forgiveness, bravery, or strength, whatever God is laying on your heart right now.

"Forget the former things; do not dwell on the past."
Isaiah 43:18

It is impossible for someone other than Jesus to meet your needs...

Just Ask the Samaritan woman at the well

Read the Samaritan woman's story: John 4:3-26

*F*rom the moment we are born, we are given the need and the desire to be loved and accepted in this world. It's the reason we say to our parents over and over, "Watch me, watch me, watch me." It's the reason we spend so much time at the field or gym, so we can show our coach we are getting better. It's the reason we are tempted to change our appearance and our personality to grab the attention of the opposite sex. And although we put on different masks to fit in and feel accepted, we really long for people to look at us and really see us; See us for who we are, not what we pretend to be. We want people to see us and still love us. We long to be noticed and validated. Unfortunately, we often seek this from everybody including coaches, parents, friends, boys, everywhere except Jesus much like the Samaritan woman. The Samaritans were a group of people that were considered outcasts, people the Jews avoided, but here was a Samaritan woman who had come to draw water from the well in the middle of the day when most of the other women come early in the morning. She was an outcast among outcasts. Why? We know she had been married five different times, and the man she was living with was not her husband. She was looking for love and acceptance in all the wrong places, but then she met Jesus. He opened her eyes to his heart. In Jesus, she found what she had been looking for, a relationship with God, the Savior of the world. She found unconditional love, acceptance, and grace. We all can!

Maybe you are working so hard in your sport to get the approval of your dad.
Maybe you are looking for love in all the wrong places.
Maybe you are looking to your friends to meet your need of acceptance.

If you relate to one or all of these, you will have unmet expectations every time. Neither your coach, your boyfriend, nor your friends were created to fulfill only that which Jesus can. He was created to meet your needs by meeting you at your well!

45

Just Ask Lauren Chamberlain
University of Oklahoma • Softball

I've always wanted to feel accepted and loved. This seems like a very
normal human desire, especially being a woman, but I struggled
heavily with needing people's approval before I came to know Christ, like
the Samaritan woman at the well. When I was eight years old, I knew
softball was going to be my sport. I was naturally talented on the field and
quickly felt accepted by my peers and coaches, based on my ability to hit
the ball far. Throughout high school and my college career, the majority
of the time I didn't see myself as Lauren, a child of God, but as Lauren,
the softball player. My identity quickly revolved around my athletic ability
and the number of fans that loved to watch me. It was the high I got from
a stranger's approval that was so satisfying, but it never seemed to last
long enough. When the lights shut off and it was time to go home after
a home game, I felt empty and the hole was wide open again, waiting
to be filled by something other than God. This is when I began to carry
the void with me into my relationships. I would look to find love and
admiration in the wrong places and with the wrong men. The excitement
of being looked at when I walked into a room replaced my insecurity. I

got into a relationship that I was settling in, and I can recall becoming physically ill if I didn't feel like I was satisfying or perfect to him. When I really met Jesus on July 15, 2014 in a baptism pool, the way I viewed myself changed forever. The Samaritan woman was an outcast. She had been married several times, and was living with a man to whom she was not married. Society looked at her a certain way based on the life she was living. Just like when the Samaritan woman left her old life at the well, I left mine in that pool. I was no longer looking to my athleticism to define me. Men no longer got to tell me if I was good enough. My chase for personal perfection turned into a chase after a perfect God. My God views me as a beautiful, strong, talented, smart woman. After feeling the Holy Spirit move within me as I came up from the water, I made a vow to stop trying to find validation from the world, and to only fix my eyes on my wonderful Creator. He continues and will always fill the void that no human can.

Just Ask Me

1) Like the Samaritan woman, who are you looking to in order to meet your needs? Boys? Coach? Friends? Parents?

2) In what area do you feel you look to others for acceptance? Emotionally? Mentally? Spiritually? Why?

3) Write a prayer asking Jesus to meet you at your well....or court.

"I have come so that you may have life and have it to the full."
John 10:10

It is possible to compete for God when the world around you does not…

Just Ask Shadrach, Meshach, and Abednego

Read Shadrach, Meshach, and Abednego's story: Daniel 3: 1-30

Some of the biggest sports news stories are those where people try to cheat or alter their body, so they can be the best in their sport or be like everyone else in their sport. And what goes on in the sports world is a direct reflection of what is going on in rest of the world. There are people willing to do anything they can to get better in this world even if it breaks the heart of God. There is cheating on every level, in every sport, but you don't have to be one of them. Athletes are tempted to lie about their age to get on a certain team. Athletes are tempted to cheat on their history test so they can be eligible to play in the game on Saturday.

Athletes are tempted not to eat for 3 days before their cheer performance so they will look better than the other girls. Let the story of these three teenagers encourage you to listen and obey God when you are tempted not to. Shadrach, Meshach, and Abednego were told by their King that they had to bow down and worship his golden statue every time they heard the music play. When everyone else in the land did as they were told, these teenage boys decided they wanted to please God rather than please people, and they refused to bow. They were made fun of, tattled on, and were even thrown in a fire. But because they chose to honor God instead of follow people, God honored them and saved them. You might be tempted to follow the crowd and do everything they are doing, but God wants you to follow him and only him. It is impossible to please everyone, but it is possible to please one…the one, God Almighty.

Just Ask Leah O'Brien-Amico
Olympic Gold medalist • USA Softball

*I*n the first few years on the USA Softball team I was learning all about God's Word (the Bible), His love, and who He says that I am as a child of God. I was even learning how to give God the glory for my talents and success on the softball field. A teammate and I would pray together before games and would talk about God with teammates when the chance came up. During the World Championships, my teammate and I both had a great game offensively. A couple girls on our team said it must have been because we prayed to God and told us that they were going to pray to their own fake god to help them. They were trying to be funny but they don't realize that they were actually mocking the God of the Bible. My teammate and I decided to pray that God would reveal Himself to them. It is not always popular to stand up for God's ways but the stand we take is important. Jesus Himself said, *"Whoever is not with me is*

against me" (Matthew 12:30). I learned through the years that God will use anyone who will stand upon His truth and will not be ashamed to share it. I sign autographs and put Philippians 4:13 under my name and many people have asked what it means or have told me that they love God too. Even signing a verse from the Bible is a way to show that I stand with God. No matter how people might try to put us down or mock our faith, God will always show up and use us in big ways to shine his light if we stand firm. I went on to win three Olympic gold medals for the USA and God has given me a bigger platform now to share how great He truly is.

Just Ask Me

1) What are some of the temptations you face as girl in the sports world?

2) The Bible says *"Two are better for one, for they have good return for their work. For if one falls down they have someone to pick them up, but pity the man that falls down and has nobody to pick them up."* (Ecclesiastes 4:9) These teenagers had each other to stand with…who can you turn to help you fight these temptations? Parents? Coach? Friends?

3) What are some action steps you are going to take today to help you play your sport for your Audience of One?

"I can do all things through Christ who gives me strength."
Philippians 4:13

We can't serve in the name of Jesus without sitting at the feet of Jesus first...

Just Ask Mary and Martha

Read Mary and Martha's story: Luke 10:38-42

*Y*ou have heard all the cliché sayings about practice and hard work…

Practice makes perfect.

Hard works beats talent when talent fails to work hard.

How you practice is how you play.

Pain is temporary, but quitting is forever.

Nobody likes practice, but everyone loves to play the game. We have to practice in order to play, however, or we will never know what to do in games. Practice is where you learn the rules, the plays, and the game plan. Without practice, there is no game.

Mary and Martha were great friends of Jesus. He would often stop at their house when he passed through their town of Bethany. This particular day, Jesus and his disciples stopped in for dinner. As far as Martha was concerned, it was game time. She was cooking, cleaning, and serving their guests, but her sister, Mary, was simply sitting and listening to Jesus teach. Martha did not understand why Jesus was not telling Mary to help her. After all, she was just doing what God had commanded…to serve one another. Jesus wanted Martha to understand what she was doing was not wrong, she was just doing it in the wrong order. We must sit before we serve. We must practice before we can play. There are so many things we want to do in the name of Jesus without sitting at his feet first. It is during this sitting time that we practice hearing his heart, his plans, and his direction for our lives before we go out and play the game of life in His name. We give so much of ourselves to others through our sport. God knows how much we need to be filled up with His strength!

Just Ask Sallie McLaurin
University of Oklahoma • Volleyball

There was an opportunity my junior year to get an internship with FCA Volleyball. I would think about it randomly over a couple of years but always thought I could not do it because I did not have enough time in the summer. It was after my busy volleyball season when we had just finished up in the NCAA's. I was sitting alone in my hotel room for the first time in a long time reading my Bible. I felt God tell me I should do the internship. I was thinking… NO WAY! So, naturally I decided to stop reading and get on Facebook. When I opened my notifications my friend, Staci Williamson, wrote on my wall. She wrote, "Hey Sallie, there is a FCA volleyball internship that I think you should be a part of."

No kidding! It was clear to me, God was trying to tell me something, and He was not going to let me miss it.

I was so consumed with trying to be the best volleyball player, teammate, and spiritual leader that I thought the team needed me during the summer. Instead of being on campus all summer, I was in California. It was very far away and allowed me to spend time with God without any distractions. Each morning we spent an hour reading scripture, journaling, and praying. It was the very first time in my life that I saw how much I needed God every single moment within the day.

During my senior year at OU, I spent an hour either in the morning or in the afternoon reading, praying, and worshiping. The times I spent with God at His feet were the highlights of my days. Alone time with God was where I found rest. When I was challenged I was able to go back to the time when I was alone with Him and was able to have courage or remind myself not to be afraid.

Before the internship, I was willing to work hard for God and wanted to please Him. I was so focused on all the good things in my life that I could do in His name that I forgot to sit down and enjoy who He is and ask Him what plans he has for me that day. Spending more time with God makes me love more because He first loved me.

Just Ask Me

1) Why is practice so important before you play?

2) What is the lesson you learned from Mary and Martha?

3) Take some time and sit with Jesus. Pray. Read. Journal.

"Then Jesus said, 'Come to me, all of you who are weary and carry heavy burdens, and I will give you rest.'"
Matthew 11:28

When we give our life over to Jesus, it doesn't mean the end of problems,
it means the end of facing problems alone...

Just ask Paul and Silas.

Read Paul and Silas' story: Acts 16:16-40.

*I*f you have ever prepared for a game, done everything right, and it still didn't turn out the way you wanted, then you can relate to Paul and Silas. They were just preaching and doing God's work and ended up beaten and thrown into jail. So often we think that once we put our faith in Jesus we shouldn't have any more problems. We have this unrealistic expectation that our life is going to be perfect all the time, and when it is not then we start questioning God, our faith in God and ourselves. This thinking is the complete opposite of what Jesus actually says. Jesus said, "I have told you these things so that in the world you will have peace. In the world, you will have trouble. But take heart! I have overcome the world." The peace doesn't come from the absence of problems but the presence of Christ. I know many of you know this already because you are sitting in the midst of trouble right now. You might be injured, your team is fighting, or your parents are going through a divorce. There are problems all around, but we don't have to face any of them alone. What does that look like? Let's Ask Paul and Silas.

"About midnight Paul and Silas were praying and singing hymns to God, and the other prisoners were listening to them." Acts 16:25
The first thing they did was pray. So often we go to our family, friends, or teammates first when God wants us to come to him first. We need to view prayer as our first option instead of our last resort.

The second thing they did was praised God in the midst of their pain. Paul and Silas had every right to be angry or bitter with God, but they teach us that when you praise God for what he has done in the past, it can help us get through our present. We are reminded that God was faithful before and He will be faithful again!

It would have been normal to praise God after they were released from jail, but they praised God while in jail. You see, when you do life with Jesus, peace comes before the answers do.

Just Ask Kelli Masters
Sports Agent and former Miss Oklahoma

*O*h, how I love the story of Paul and Silas declaring their trust in God in the middle of a seemingly hopeless situation! When they could have focused on their pain, they instead looked to God and sang praises to Him. Their choices in that moment affected not only their own lives but also the lives of everyone else in that prison—and countless others who have read their story throughout history.

If you know about Paul, you know that he was an adult when he first encountered Jesus personally and experienced a radical life change. He had been very religious, but when Jesus appeared to him on the road to Damascus, everything changed! Like Paul, I did not come to know Jesus until my early twenties. While growing up I attended church, called myself a Christian and knew about Jesus. But I did not truly know Him as my personal Lord and Savior until later. So I remember life before him. What a roller coaster of emotions! When good things happened, I was happy and excited. But when difficulties came, I found myself empty and in despair.

During a particularly difficult time, when I was breaking off an engagement and questioning my purpose in life, I cried out to God for help. And that is when I discovered Jesus as a real person! I realized Jesus was crazy in love with me and had taken on all my mistakes and shame because of that love. When He gave His life on the cross, He was saving mine and giving me hope. And real hope does not come and go depending on what is happening in your life. It is forever!

After giving my life to Christ, my circumstances did not become easier. Bad things still happened, people still hurt me and things didn't always work out the way I wanted. But there was one MASSIVE difference; I had PEACE. In every trial, I can stay strong and full of joy and hope because I trust in God. And He is always with me, working things out in my favor. I may not always see the answer or the victory right away, but I know it is coming. He is ALWAYS faithful because he loves me. And He loves YOU the same way!

Just Ask Me

1) What are the biggest problems you are facing right now?

2) How do you handle your struggles, fear, and/or pain?

3) How has the story of Paul and Silas encouraged you as a female and an athlete?

"This is confidence we have in approaching God: that if we ask anything according to his will, he hears us."
1 John 5:14

Just Ask Ruth

Read Ruth's story: Ruth 1-4

As girls, we are always being told how to make ourselves more attractive and more appealing to different people, from boys to college coaches. We are told how to do our hair, how to dress, and what to fix in our sport. So many of the changes people want us to make deal with the physical, when God wants us to address the spiritual. So often we address the body, when God wants us to address the heart.

We are going to look at the qualities of a girl named Ruth and how her story will encourage you in yours. Ruth was married to one of Naomi's sons. After both Naomi's husband and sons died, she was left with no other option than to return to her homeland. She encouraged her daughter in law, Ruth, to return to her homeland as well, but this is our first glimpse into the heart of Ruth.

Ruth replied, "Don't ask me to leave you and turn back. Wherever you go, I will go; wherever you will live, I will live. Your people will be my people, and your God will be my God." Ruth 1:16

Her loyalty and kindness didn't stop there. She returned with her mother in law and worked each day gathering the leftover grain the harvesters dropped just so she could feed herself and Naomi. The man in whose field she was working in took notice of her, not her looks, but her heart. "The Lord bless you…you are showing more family loyalty now than you did before…" Ruth 3:10

The man asked her to marry him and they became descendants of King David and eventually Jesus! Ruth didn't just focus on her appearance to get a relationship, she worked on her heart to get the right one. We work so hard to fit into this world when God wants us to stand out. Be different in how you act on the court. Be different in how you treat your teammates. Be different in how you view being attractive. Paul says it this way in 1 Timothy 4:7-8, "Do not waste time arguing over godless ideas and old wives tales. Instead train yourself to be godly. Physical training is good, but training for godliness is much better, promising benefits in this life and in the life to come."

Two of the most attractive qualities are loyalty and kindness… just ask Ruth.

Just Ask Brianna Way

University of Oklahoma • Soccer and Softball

College was a time of growth, a time of change and a time of searching for the woman that God has created me to be. When I was seventeen years old I moved from my home and family in California to start a new adventure at the University of Oklahoma. It was a culture shock for me. Honestly, my first couple of years I acted like I had it all together. I acted like Christ was the center of my life, acted like my outward appearance honored Christ, but in reality, my heart did not. There was a point in my college career that I questioned who I really was, who I wanted to be, and more importantly who God wanted me to be. As a college athlete you are put on a pedestal and there are expectations that coaches, teammates and even fans will hold you to. They are expectations that may make you a little uncomfortable, uneasy, and those that test your ability to overcome adversities. Throughout my first couple years in college I was trying to fill these expectation in the wrong ways. I was going out, drinking, and trying to be the teammate, girlfriend and friend that my peers wanted me to be. I was searching for the right way to meet their standards.

It was the times that should fill me up, according to the world, that would leave my heart feeling empty. I would sit in my apartment and wonder why meeting these expectations did not fill my heart. It was then I realized that I was missing Christ. I focused so much on what I looked like to people, and made sure I was representing what people wanted me to be, that I neglected Christ. My heart was empty although I had so much. Jesus is enough. A lot of people think living with freedom means to go out and enjoy the things of this world, but living for Jesus introduces you to true freedom, and that is where I found mine. Like Ruth, I want people to see my heart because that is where God lives.

Just Ask Me

1) What is the hardest part of being a female athlete in today's world?

2) Write Paul's words in 2 Timothy 2 in your own words.

3) What did you learn from Ruth?

"Charm is deceptive, beauty is fleeting, but a woman who fears the Lord is to be praised."

Proverbs 31:30

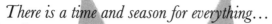

There is a time and season for everything…

Just Ask Esther

Read Esther's Story: Esther 1-7

*I*n sports we often talk about our in-season and our off-season, but let's be honest, there really is no off-season. You are just doing something different in off-season in preparation for your in-season. There is purpose in every season. Preparing yourself to get faster and stronger in one or preparing your skills in another. You can't have one season without the other…they work together.

Esther had to learn this lesson of God's timing and preparation when her people were on the verge of getting eliminated by the King's evil sidekick, Haman. Esther was made queen of Persia, but she was of Jewish descent. After learning of Haman's plan to exterminate the entire Jewish community, Esther's cousin pleaded with her to use her position as Queen to save their people. He asked her this question, "Who knows if perhaps you were made queen for just such a time as this?" Esther 4:14

The Bible teaches us in Ecclesiastes 3:1, "For everything there is a season, a time for every activity under heaven." There was a season of preparation for Esther, a time to prepare her heart, mind, and body to become Queen of Persia. Then there was what all the preparation led up to, a time to use her position as queen to save her people as a Jew. Just like our sport, God has a plan, a purpose, and season for everything we do:

- A time to prepare and a time to play.
- A time to plant and a time to harvest.
- A time to hurt and a time to heal.

I don't know what season of life you are in right now; it may be good or it may be a struggle. You may be in a season of waiting, wondering, or wishing God would show himself. I want to encourage you that while you are waiting, God is working. While you are preparing, God is planning. Find hope in the story of Esther that God is preparing you for "such a time as this."

Just Ask Jennifer Sharpe

Former Trainer for University of Connecticut and current wife and mom

*S*eems like there is no off-season anymore. Certainly I see that in our lives. My husband is a head athletic trainer for an NBA team. He has been doing this for many years, and prior to working with professional athletes, he spent nine years with a Division I basketball program. He has also been a part of international competition with USA Basketball. This is my story, though, and how my purpose in life has changed from what I planned.

I emerged from graduate school with a dream to be an athletic trainer for elite collegiate athletes, and I landed what should have been the perfect position. Life happened, though, and I met my now-husband. As opportunity for him grew, I found my career plans unraveling. The demands of his job and schedule made it necessary for me to be more stable and available to manage our home, which became even more evident as we started our family.

I wish that I could say that those early years of our marriage were all honeymoon bliss. The sad truth is that it was very hard for me as I transitioned from one career path to another, from full time to part time, in the work force, to full time motherhood. Many days I found myself repeatedly asking God, "Why? What is my role in all this?" My identity was lost somewhere in dirty diapers and laundry.

But God is faithful, and He has a purpose for all of us, even if it is hard to see in the midst of darkness. During the tough times, I opened my Bible and met Esther. The wise words of counsel that Mordecai offered Esther have become my creed. Perhaps all the trials that I have been through, the different seasons of life, the highs and lows, have all been for such a time as this?

I have found peace in the Word. My job is to be at my husband's side, for my steadfastness helps gives him strength. My job is to be the rock that provides for my two children, acting as both mom and dad when necessary. I recently entered a new season of life, the phase of motherhood known as "the time when all the children go to school." My extra time has allowed me to forge a new career path in a variety of paid and volunteer positions, service and ministry, industry and charity.

In the moments of doubt and uncertainty, I repeat my mantra from Esther. I am walking with Jesus as a wife, mother and citizen of the world for "such a time is this."

Just Ask Me

1) What is the hardest part of off-season for you?

2) What season of life would you say you are in right now?

3) How were you encouraged by the story of Esther?

"Yet God has made everything beautiful for its own time."
Ecclesiastes 3:11

When you are running with God, you can't help but overhear your purpose in God...

Just Ask Isaiah

Read Isaiah's story: Isaiah 6:1-9

*W*ouldn't you just love to know what God has in store for your future? What kind of year will you have? Will you get hurt this year? Will you play in college? Will you ever get married and to whom? We have so many questions that we want God to answer right now. I love that God is all-knowing. He knows that if he shows us what will happen tomorrow, we will miss what he wants us to know today. So what do we do in the meantime? Do not try to figure out your future, get to know the one who created it. Isaiah was a prophet in the Old Testament who was simply in the presence of God and overheard a need of God. Isaiah 6:8 says, "Then I heard the Lord asking, 'Whom should I send as a messenger to this people? Who will go for us?'" Isaiah replied to God, "Here I am. Send me." God wasn't asking Isaiah to go. God wasn't telling Isaiah to go. Because Isaiah was searching for God through prayer, he encountered God's plans. God wants us all to do the same.

• He wants us to spend time alone with Him.
• He might want you to lead a bible study for your team.
• He wants you to be a Christ-like influence on your team.
• He wants you to use your influence to share the gospel.

We find out what He wants when we find out who He is. We do this by reading His Word, Praying to His heart, and engaging with His followers. Get to know God because your future plans are in His hands.

Just Ask Dayna Huckabee
Arkansas • Softball

*T*he fear of the unknown. I've faced this giant several times in my Christian walk. My first encounter happened shortly after my career as a softball player at the University of Arkansas. During my career, it was through the influence of a teammate and a campus minister that I saw Christ lived out in ways I had never experienced before. I saw the power of influence through loving, selfless relationships and I wanted to have the same impact on young women's lives. I started working for FCA in 2010. I felt like I was on top of the world. I had my dream job, at my dream school and life couldn't have been any better. But then the storm came, and it was a big one. Before I had even completed my first year of ministry, my mother was diagnosed with cancer and died a quick two and a half months later. My world stopped. I was crushed. I didn't know how to continue. Everything that once seemed so certain and so true was all unclear. I had no idea what the future would hold for me. I felt like I was in a 50 foot deep hole with no way out. I tried to be strong enough. I tried to depend on other people. I tried shutting down. None of it worked. A few months after, I was put in a position of sole leadership of FCA on campus, and I was terrified. I thought the ministry was going to tank. "What am I going to do? How am I going to reach all of these athletes for Christ?" Doubts flooded my mind. I was beat down, defeated, and almost to the point where I was going to quit. Then, God stepped in and reminded me that I didn't have to have it all figured out. All I needed to do was focus on growing in my relationship with Him. Every uncertainty that was a result of my Mom's death, ministry questions, or struggles in life were all put to rest as I found myself trusting in the one who is sovereign over all. I was set free knowing that I didn't have to have it all figured out. I could see clearly, even though some things were still yet to be seen. I am confident now that no matter what uncertainty life throws at me, how crazy my circumstances are, or how much I doubt, I can always stand firm in the truth of God's word and the promise of His presence. This alone has sustained me through the deepest, darkest, most painful moments in my life, and it will continue to be my firm foundation.

Just Ask Me

1) What future plans do you wish God would tell you right now?

2) As a student athlete your schedule can be crazy. What can you do to make sure you spend more time with God?

3) Write a Prayer to God about your dreams, your future, and His plans.

"You can make many plans, but the Lord's purpose will prevail."
Proverbs 19:21

If your opponent can get you to doubt your identity then he can get you to doubt your purpose…

Just Ask Jesus

Read Jesus's story: Matthew 3:13-17, 4:1-11

*T*he art of talking trash to your opponent has taken over the sports world. It's the tactic of trying to get your opponents discouraged and doubting themselves so that you can win the competition before it even starts. Jesus had an opponent that tried to do just this, bring him down before he even began his ministry. We read in Matthew 3:13-17 that right before Jesus met his opponent, God declared him "my dearly loved Son, who brings me great joy." And the first thing his opponent, Satan, does is try to get Jesus to doubt himself by saying, "if you are the son of God…." Once we make a commitment to be followers of Jesus, His enemy becomes our enemy. He whispers the same trash talking garbage in our ears in attempt to doubt who we are in Christ. It may sound like this… "if you are child of God," "if you're not a failure," "if you are forgiven," all words that are not anything God has told us we are through his son, Jesus. Romans 8:15-16 says, "So you have not received a spirit that makes you fearful slaves. Instead, you received God's Spirit when he adopted you has his own children. Now we call him, "Abba, Father." For His spirit joins with our spirit to affirm that we are God's children."

We are daughters of the King, a part of His Kingdom, but if our opponent can get us to doubt our identity then he can get us to doubt our purpose. Our purpose is to do great things for God with the talents we have been given by God.

Karen Wheaton said it this way, "Satan's greatest fear is that you would believe what God says about you." We defeat our enemy, our opponent, the same way Jesus did, by believing God and who he says we are. You ARE a child of God because HE says so. You ARE forgiven because HE says "In Christ we are set free by the blood of his death, and so we have forgiveness of sins." You ARE NOT a failure because He says "there is no condemnation for those who are in Christ Jesus." Know the truth and the truth will set you free.

Just Ask Becca Clark

USA Junior and University of Oklahoma Gymnastics Team

I am currently in the last few months of my gymnastics career. I have been doing gymnastics for almost 20 years now, starting when I was just three years old. I have loved it from my very first class. As the years passed my training gradually became more intense, and by the time I reached fifth grade I was spending 40 plus hours a week in the gym. I still loved every minute of it. In high school I had the opportunity to represent the United States in competitions. With that opportunity to wear red, white, and blue on my leotard came pressure, responsibility, and pride. I can't say when exactly it started to happen, but at some point along the way I began to find my identity in gymnastics.

Little did I know that my freshman year as a Sooner, God was going to intervene. I knew what an honor it was to wear Sooners across my back and couldn't wait to represent the University of Oklahoma. Halfway through my freshman competition season, I suffered a knee injury that not many can come back from. I dislocated my right knee, tearing my ACL and LCL along with other damage. That was my rock bottom. I had always been a gymnast, always; the one thing that I had been identifying as was taken away. For the time being, I couldn't be a gymnast. So who or what was I?

My rock bottom was where God started to rebuild my identity, only this time it was in Him. God had other plans for me after that year and has allowed me to have an amazing career at OU so far, including both, winning a team National Championship, and becoming an All American. God has also used my sport as a platform to glorify Him and share His love with others. Gymnastics has been and always will be a huge part of my life because God has used it to teach me so many lessons and give me countless experiences and opportunities. Gymnastics is what I do though, it is not who I am. I am a daughter of the one true King.

The devil is going to fight the hardest when God is up to something great. For me the devil came in the form of something I loved and that God had given me a passion and work ethic for and he got me to believe that it defined me. There is only one identity that is eternal and will never let you down, will never change, and will never fail you, that is your identity in God.

Just Ask Me

1) What lies from your opponent have you been believing about yourself?

2) Write down some "truth" of who God says you are.

3) Write a prayer asking God to help you defeat your opponent.

"And since we are his children, we are his heirs. In fact, together with Christ we are heirs of God's glory."
Romans 8:17

Just Ask Judas

Read Judas' story: Matthew 26: 14-30,
47-36 and Matthew 27:5

*T*here is one thing every coach wants and needs from their players. It's the one thing every coach looks for and asks above all else. It's not talent. It's not strength. It's not speed. It's to be coachable. Being coachable is putting your own agenda aside to listen to your coach for the good of the team. Listen to what you are doing wrong and be willing to change it. Take what your coach is saying as constructive criticism and use it to get better...to be better. This is not an easy task to accomplish because it means we have to get out of the way. It means we have to put our personal agendas aside out of respect for the coach and the team.

Judas was one of Jesus' 12 disciples. He was part of the team, the inner circle. He watched Jesus perform miracles and listened to Him teach day after day. He heard Jesus' words, but never let them penetrate his heart. His personal agenda led him to betray Jesus and what could have been his personal savior. He gave up a life with Jesus for money. Sounds crazy right? We do it all the time. We give up life with Jesus for our sport, popularity, or acceptance from the world. We choose the things of this world that we think will make us happy over the one thing that actually will, relationship with Jesus.

Let us learn from Judas that we can't be coached by Jesus if we aren't willing to get out of the way. Our own personal agendas and need for control can keep us from fully surrendering to our ultimate head coach, Jesus! It is His game plan that gives us life to the full, not ours. Jesus said, "If you cling to your life, you will lose it; but if you give up your life for me, you will find it." Matthew 10:39...Judas was living proof.

Just Ask Samantha Ricketts
University of Oklahoma • Softball

*A*s a collegiate softball coach, I work with many talented players every
day. They all have different skills and abilities, but coachable is a descrip-
tion that comes up often. The coachable characteristic is more than just
doing what a coach asks. It is listening, responding, and making everyone
around you better. If a player cannot find that willingness to trust what
they do not know, they may be missing out on an even greater unknown
if they would just trust the process.

As a high school senior trying to decide the next stage of my life, I
had to make a decision to trust God and the unknown and be uncomfortable doing so. Growing up in San Jose, CA, I had already decided to
play softball for the school right down the road from my high school. It
was close, it was comfortable, and it was really the only scholarship offer
I had so I was thankful.

Then a month before school started, the coach who recruited me
quit, and another opportunity appeared. I was offered a chance to
play softball for the University of Oklahoma. This was an opportunity
beyond anything I could imagine. OU had been to the Women's College
World Series for five straight years. They had one of the best coaches in
the country in Patty Gasso.

But I had to decide in a week. Without visiting the school, without meeting anyone in the program. It was one of the most daunting moments of my life. I literally had to look up the state of Oklahoma on a map because I had no idea where it was. I thought OU was the black and orange school in the state, which I later learned is a big NO, that is rival Oklahoma State. At 18 years old I had a decision to make: follow my comfortable plan and stay close to home, or move halfway across the country by myself and face the unknown and truly challenge myself to play with and against the best. It was not an easy decision; my parents tried to stay out of my way so they would not influence me to stay close, which is what they wanted.

It was the first time I really broke down and cried, praying for God to lead me to make the right decision, the decision that would be following His plan for me. I ended up getting out of God's way and trusting Him; I went to Oklahoma and became a two-time All American. More importantly, I found my relationship with Jesus. I learned about FCA and became a leader in the group on campus. I brought other friends along with me. That one decision shaped everything about my life, my faith, and even guided me to my career now, coaching. I can use my influence to encourage other players to now make the tough choices and lean on God in those times, all because I surrendered to His will.

Just Ask Me

1) When is a time you put your personal agenda before the team?

2) How do you put the things of this world before the things of God?

3) Judas teaches us that you can be in the presence of God and miss God. Don't miss God! Write a personal prayer to God.

"But if anyone obeys his word, love for God is truly made complete in them. This is how we know we are in him: whoever claims to live in him must live as Jesus did."
1 John 2:5-6

Just Ask Paul

Read Paul's Story: Acts 9:1-31

*I*n sports, there is always a scoreboard. You keep score in softball, basketball, volleyball, gymnastics etc. It's the one way to know who is winning and who is losing. Unfortunately, we often take this same scoring system into our relationship with God. If we have done a bad thing, then we have to do something good to make up for it. As long as we do more good than bad, we should be okay with God. Right? Wrong! Paul teaches us this very important lesson through his words and his story. Paul was a man who persecuted Christians with more than just his words, but his actions too. His rap sheet included beatings, murder, and hate. After he became a follower of Jesus Christ, he writes in his letter to Ephesus, "God saved you by his grace when you believed. And you can't take credit for this; it is a gift from God. Salvation is not a reward for the good things we have done so none of us can boast about it." Ephesians 2:8-9 It's not the "good" that go to heaven, it's the perfect and not one of us can say we are perfect, that is why we need Jesus. That is the gift of salvation!

With that being said, it doesn't mean we shouldn't still do good things. Paul writes to his friend Timothy, "Don't let anyone look down on you because you are young, but set an example in speech, life, love, faith and purity." 1 Timothy 4:12

Good works do not lead to salvation, but they can lead to a positive influence. When you say you are a Christian, people watch. They watch how you talk, act, and react. The influence you have is a direct reflection of the salvation you received. We do good things not to get love from God but out of love for God. We do because God did!

Just Ask Laura Clay
Hall of Fame Cross Country Coach

I was lucky. I did not know that, but I was. I came in to the world with a twin sister and a wonderful family of loving parents and siblings. I was so fortunate. My parents demonstrated, modeled and taught all of us the lessons of life. One of the core lessons my parents impressed on me was the work ethic. My dad and mom worked hard every day. My dad spent countless hours on the road as a long haul truck driver. My mom spent endless days in the health care profession taking care of others. I thought working hard was what you were supposed to do—working hard was what they modeled for me every day. As I began my athletic career as a runner I saw that this work ethic was very valuable in competition. The harder I worked at running the more success I experienced. Work hard, be successful—a great lesson for life. As a young coach, I repeated the process. The harder I work, the more I do, the greater the chance is for my team to be successful.

My spiritual life began much the same way....I was lucky. I was around people that exposed me to the love of God. As a result of the direction I received as a young person, I accepted Christ as my Savior. I thought my relationship with my Heavenly Father would be very similar…work hard and be successful. I admit, I approached my spiritual life as I had my family life and athletic life—work hard for God and I can be successful in my relationship with Him.

What I didn't understand and couldn't get my head around was that God loved me, not my works. His explanation in Ephesians 2:8 says "it was by grace through faith" and not by works! Now, for a working girl that was hard to swallow, but it was the truth. It was His Gift to mankind. It was all I needed. He is going to give me salvation no matter how hard I work because He loves me for me and not because of how hard I work.

I told you I was lucky…when my husband and I would make long road trips, we enjoy the time together by sharing a book—he would drive and I would read. The book I read to him that day on a trip home from Dallas after a marathon is now my favorite book of all time, Max Lucado's *The Grip of Grace*. For the first time in my life, by reading out loud Lucado's words, I finally understood the power of God's grace. God's grace, not our works……God's Love, not our actions, is all we need. Period! Our lives changed that day. We are saved by grace not by works but for good works. I still believe in hard work, and I coach my athletes to develop the work ethic I was taught as a child, but my relationship with my Heavenly Father is now clear to me—our relationship is based on His Grace.

Just Ask Me

1) How do you use a scoreboard when it comes to your relationship with God?

2) Write your definition of Grace.

3) How can you set a positive example in your speech, life, love, faith and purity?

"I have given you an example to follow. Do as I have done for you."
John 13:15

God can do more with a little than you can do with a lot…

Just Ask Gideon

Read Gideon's story: Judges 6 & 7

*E*veryone loves stories of the underdog. We love movies like *Rudy, Miracle,* and *Invincible* because they are the stories of ordinary people that do extraordinary things. They give us hope, encouragement, and inspiration that maybe, just maybe, we could do something great too. One of the greatest underdog stories in the Bible is that of a man named Gideon. During the time of Gideon, his people, the Israelites, had been taken over by the Midianites and lived under their savage rules for 7 years. The Israelites cried out to God for help, and God went to Gideon. "The Lord turned to him and said, "Go in the strength you have and save Israel out of Midian's hand. Am I not sending you?" (Judges 6:14)

Only Gideon was not a general in the army. He wasn't a leader among the people. Actually, Gideon was farming wheat when God made this request. Self-doubt found its way into Gideon's mind and out his mouth. "But how can I save Israel? My clan is the weakest in Manasseh, and I am the least in my family." (Judges 6:15)

According to the world, and Gideon, he was a simple farmer, weak and unable to do anything strong. To God, though, he was a "mighty warrior." (Judges 6:12). Gideon teaches us that God can use anybody, at any time, to do anything. Why not you? You think you are too slow…God is with you, mighty warrior. You think you can't conquer your fears….God is with you, mighty warrior. You think you will never make it through this tough season…God is with you mighty warrior. Something weak in God's hand is more than all the strength in yours! God helped Gideon win His battle and he is just waiting to help you in yours!

Just Ask Melissa Wolff
Arkansas • Basketball

*I*t was my junior year in high school, and my dream was to play college basketball. There was only one problem; I didn't have any scholarship offers yet. My coach talked to several small division I colleges, but they all said I was too slow and not good enough to play at their level. The summer before my senior year I played for the best AAU team in the state and played in front of hundreds of college scouts at exposure tournaments. Because God had a plan for me greater than I could've ever imagined for myself, I was offered a full scholarship to the school of my dreams, the University of Arkansas.

This was only the beginning of a great journey ahead of me. I felt God calling me to be a leader for my team, but thousands of doubts flooded my mind: "I'm only a freshman, I'm not even good enough to play here, Why would anyone listen to, much less follow me?" As I struggled with these doubts ad fears throughout the year I stumbled across 2 Corinthians 12:9 "My grace is sufficient for you, My power is made perfect in weakness." God didn't need my talents or whatever qualification I thought I had to be a leader. He simply needed me to be available and trust that He was going to work. I had the opportunity to play at the highest level of college basketball and be a leader for this team the past two years, not because of anything I did but because when God works through you, you can accomplish so much more than you ever will on your own.

Just Ask Me

1) What are some areas in your life you think you are weak?

2) What self-doubt creeps into your mind in your sport?

3) How does the story of Gideon inspire you?

*"The angel of the Lord appeared to him and said,
'Mighty warrior, the Lord is with you!'"*
Judges 6:12

There is no gift or talent that is insignificant...

Just Ask the boy with Two fish and Five loaves of bread

Read The boy's story: Matthew 14:13-21

*W*hen a little boy left his house one morning, he left with a lunch. It was a simple lunch that his momma packed him, something that just seemed insignificant and ordinary. He went to listen to a teacher that day named Jesus. But on this day, the boy's ordinary lunch was put into the hands of an extraordinary God. Jesus asked the disciples what food they had to feed the people and they pointed to this little boy who had two fish and five loaves of bread. To the boy, to the people, and to the disciples what he had to offer just seemed insignificant. Gifts in the hands of man can be insignificant, but gifts in the hands of God can change the world. Jesus told them to do something, and their reply was, "BUT Jesus we only have this to offer, it is of no significance" Jesus says bring me what you have and watch me work.

He wants to do the same for you and me. Did you know that you have been given a gift and/or talent by God to be used for God? Yes...You! It is hard to see our own gifts when others around us seem to have much better gifts...right? Maybe you don't think it is significant because you are not the leading scorer. Maybe you are called a "role player," and you have no idea what that means. Maybe you can't possibly see what you have to offer to the team. As humans, we tend to put gifts in categories: good, better, best. The ones that have more visibility are more important. But God doesn't see gifts with more visibility any more significant those gifts that are behind the scenes. 1 Corinthians 12:4-7 says, "There are different types of spiritual gifts, but the same Spirit is the source of them all. There are different kinds of service, but we serve the same Lord. God works in different ways, but it is the same God who does the work in all of us..."

As a follower of Christ you have been given a gift, not for you, but for God...so He can use you, mold you, and minister to you. He just wants to know that you are using them to your full capability and for His glory, not for yours.

If God can feed over 5,000 people with two fish and 5 loaves of bread, just imagine what He can do with your gift...if you bring it to Him.

You can do one of three things with the gift God has given you: Hide it, Resent it, or *Bring it.*

Just Ask Sarah Roberts

I am from a small town in the Oklahoma panhandle that doesn't even have a stop light. I was an average basketball player that played one year of college ball before I got married. I am married to a football coach, and we have five kids. There is nothing extraordinary about me, so when God first put it on my heart to write a devotion book, I ignored him. Why? Because who was I? I didn't have anything good to say, but then God gently whispered…I do.

- "But God, all I have is the lessons I have learned from you in my journal"…Sarah, bring me what you have and watch me work.
- "But God, I have made bad decisions in the past and am not worthy to be used" …Sarah, bring me what you have and watch me work.
- "But God, I am not a writer"…Sarah, bring me what you have and watch me work.

Once I decided God is God and I am not Him, I put the idea out there. The fears and doubts shortly followed. I have never really thought of myself as an insecure person. Ever since I became a follower of Christ at an FCA camp in 1993, I found my identity in Jesus…or so I thought. All it took was this little devotion book to show me that I do fear what people think. I do doubt that God would use me. I do have fears that I will fail. I have realized I have always had these emotions, God has just used this little project of His to bring them to the surface, out my eyes, and onto my bathroom floor. And let me tell you…God has plowed through every fear, anxious thought, and insecurity. I am like this boy who simply had two fish and five loaves and was willing to put them into the hands of God…and watch Him work.

Just Ask Me

1) How do you view your role on the team? Overwhelming? Insignificant?

2) Read 2 Corinthians 12:12-30. How do the gifts God has given followers of Jesus work according to this passage?

3) What are some actual steps you need to do in order to Bring your gifts to Jesus? Pray about it? Talk to someone? Make an action plan?

"All of you together are Christ's body, and each of you is a part of it."
1 Corinthians 12:27